W9-AYP-926

Advance Praise for
The House of Sages

In *The House of Sages*, surely one of the year's best books of
poetry, Philip Terman reminds us of the responsibilities we
have to the past, the "beloved dead" of family and tribe,
nation and faith whose voices reach us when we listen for
them. (And no one writes about the world of fathers and sons
with greater insight and sensitivity than Terman.) These wise,
carefully crafted poems explore, in all its varieties, the nature
of love.

—*David Citino*

Philip Terman's poems, like those of James Wright, have a
down-to-earth mysticism, a hard-earned spirituality which
cuts through the haze of the everyday. This collection is
remarkable for its range, depth, and mature vision. From the
moving portrait of his father the used car salesman to his
gentle meditations on rural Pennsylvania, Terman captures
the heart of people, and the heart of places....

—*Jim Daniels*

Philip Terman's *The House of Sages* has the clear focus and
clean lines of good poetry, but its real and telling rituals are
based in its stories, vignettes, pieces of personal histories,
sequences and painful meditations—in its narrative of the
Jewish immigrant interrogation of the sins of and inheritance
from the fathers. And of lessons learned and unlearned, and
of the wisdom of the Torah handed down, understood. The
fact that the setting for the poems is mid-western and
pastoral only adds to the resonance of innocence confronted.
Terman's writing is rich with the need to convey his confron-
tations and affections, and not simply in the striking detail
but in the whole moment of his memory.

—*Stanley Plumly*

Philip Terman writes with passion and compassion about the
subjects close to his heart: his love for family of origin, his
wife, and his Jewish heritage. These poems, written in an
eloquent but wry voice, takes us on a journey from Terman's
father's used car lot in Cleveland back to the old world *shtetl*.
Along the way, *The House of Sages* shows us what it means to
be your father's son, to connect with your ancestry, and to
puzzle over the precise words that ground us in this life and
that propel us into the next.

—*Mary Swander*

The House of Sages

The House of Sages

poems by Philip Terman

MAMMOTH books
DuBois, Pennsylvania

Copyright © 1998 by Philip Terman

All rights reserved. No part of this book may be reproduced
in any manner without written permission from the pub-
lisher, except for brief quotations used in reviews or critical
articles.

MAMMOTH press inc.
c/o LaBue Printing inc.
140 McCracken Run Road
DuBois, Pennsylvania 15801

Cover photo "Casting Away Sins," by Julie M. Elman
Design by Antonio Vallone
Production by LaBue Printing inc., DuBois, Pennsylvania

Library of Congress Catalog Card Number: 98-87194

ISBN 0-9666028-1-1

First edition

A special thanks to Kay Fineran Luthin, Judy Rock and
all the other sages for their invaluable help
in the preparation of this book.

Acknowledgments

Cadakoin Review	"Mourners' Kaddish"
The Cream City Review:	"English as a Second Language"
Heart Quarterly:	"Oil City Serenade"
The Kenyon Review:	"One Day This Will All Be Yours" "Our Only Guarantee" "A Cast of Thousands" "Intensive Care"
The Laurel Review:	"Home Movie: The *Bris*"
The Mid-American Review:	"From the Heartland" "Without Closure"
The Midwest Quarterly:	"In This Hour of Privacy"
The Nebraska Review:	"Swallows" "My Father Calls My Name in the Voice of a Bird"
The New England Review:	"The *Shvitz*"
Nimrod:	"For Ganya"
The North American Review:	"In Cather Country"
The Ohio Journal:	"Jokes from the Depression" "Upon Leaving Martins Ferry, Ohio"
The Pittsburgh Post-Gazette:	"Meditation in Winter"
The Pittsburgh Quarterly:	"Meditation in Oil City, Pennsylvania"
Poet and Critic:	"For Etheridge Knight"
Poetry:	"G-d" "My Father's Mother"

"Eloquence"
"Attachments"
"The House of Sages"
"What We Pass On"
"Yom Kippur"

Poetry Northwest: "Instructions on Climbing Your
                           Father's Garage"
                       "Child of God"

Prairie Schooner: "Some Days"
                       "For Irina Ratushinskaya"
                       "The Wounds"
                       "The Oldest Brother Lesson in
                           the World"
                       "The Book of the World"
                       "Poem in Search of Perfection"

Slipstream: "A Prayer for Jackie Gleason"

The Southern Poetry Review: "The Story of Fathers
                                   and Sons"
                              "What Survives"

Response: "Ritual"

Tar River Poetry: "If We Were as Brilliant as
                           Groundhogs"

Tikkun: "The Synagogue in Oil City,
                           Pennsylvania"

West Branch: "Saturday Night Blues Hour"
                       "Isaiah at Rest"

Some of these poems appeared in the chapbook *What Survives,* published by Sow's Ear Press, 1993.

"Swallows" and "My Father Calls My Name in the Voice of a Bird" were nominated for a Pushcart Prize.

"For Ganya" was a finalist for the Pablo Neruda Poetry Award, sponsored by *Nimrod.*

For my mother, Mildred,
In memory of my father, Joseph,
and...for Ganya

Contents

One: The Used Car Lot

Two: Attachments

Three: Houses

Four: Sages

The House of Sages

One:

The Used Car Lot

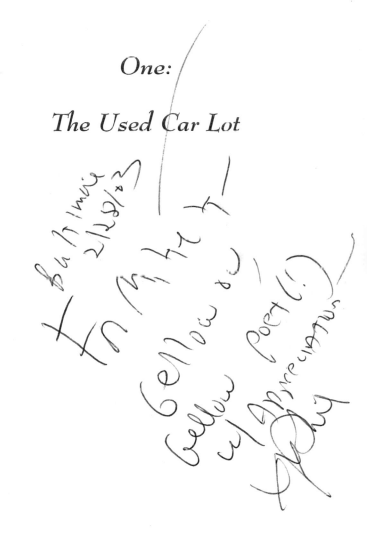

The Used Car Lot

1. One Day This Will All Be Yours

I don't fall in love
with any of them, my father says,
his back hunched
over the titles on his desk,
the butt-end of the cigar

he can't smoke at home
torn as a crumpled dollar bill.
During the riots
the place was torched,
the neighborhood clogged

like arteries
in the year of the heart attack.
Now, pennants hanging from wires
in rows above the cars
cough dust into Cleveland humidity.

My father tells me to wash
the frontline, claims
I think manual labor
is a Mexican. A customer arrives,
looks over a brown Dodge.

It's good transportation, he says.
He sold one without an engine once.
I hose a hood
clean of pollution
that splotches everywhere.

Back in the office, over gin rummy,
my father sweeps his eyes
over his rented property:
One day this will all be yours.
He picks up the gut card

I throw him, places it gently
into his spread, slides it down
with his elbow, pauses,
and gins.
Didn't I tell you never to speculate?

2. Ritual

Early each morning
before we woke for real,
I would stand and wait
in the hallway outside
the bathroom door, opened
a crack just large enough
for me to see the outline
of my father's blue pajamas
leaning in the breaking dawn light,
his elbows resting above the tank
of the toilet, too tired to stand up straight.
                    Come on in,
he would whisper, my own small
pressure burning. I added
to his steady rush and wondered
how I would ever do so much growing:
it takes two hands to handle a whopper,
he'd say, and I'd chuckle,
our only conversation in the brief
ritual we exchanged at the same
hour in that chamber, touching as never
during the day, the secret we told no one.

3. Our Only Guarantee

The cars face Euclid Avenue
in uneven rows,
wise in their junk frames.

The bodyman wheels them in,
removes rust, spray paints,
assigns each a place:

in front—'68 Pontiac,
'73 Olds, '66 Caddy,
pink, with A.C.,

'80 Mustang with music,
in back—the junkers
that won't turn over,

weeds jetting out of fenders,
hoods, trunks, doors, open to give
one more spare part: jack and hubcap,

radiator and radio.
Each is priced *As Is*.
Our only guarantee is to the curb.

Used and sold, used and sold,
spun down countless highways,
driven beyond their limits,

stalled, abandoned
just after the breakdowns,
how did they congregate

in this gravel yard
like pilgrims gathered
at the Holy Land?

4. Terman Motors Special

Every weekday morning my father drives
from one new car dealership to another:
Spitzer Cadillac, Kenny Lincoln Mercury,
Schwartz Oldsmobile, Crestmont Chevrolet,

looking for merchandise. The showroom
he is swallowed into is all space and lights
gleaming at the latest models, American-made,
gigantic in their angled displays, reflecting

his figure in the glisten of their new spit shine.
Does he wonder how they can be made
so beautiful—glazed Milky White or Sun Yellow
or Rose Red or Deep Sky Blue like glossy photos?

But these are real and he can walk around one,
he can even touch it—the latest Cadillac—can move
his hand along its chrome and caress its hood
and know no scratch or chipped edge or rust spot—

a perfection he understands is impossible in this life.
He doesn't look up but walks past this year's models,
then last year's, then all the years before that, steered
by forces that keep him in steady alignment toward

those that need a tire changed, a jump start, parked
in back, marked by patches of grass and gravel
and a tree without leaves where they store stock for parts:
bent-up has-beens rusting like farm equipment left

to weather long after their owners have moved away,
most of them ordinary and nondescript, dull browns
and drab olive greens, good for getting from here
to there, dependable in their day: Dusters and Demons

and Darts, Pintos and Omnis and Chevy Vegas, cars
with reconstructed parts from chopshops, except
for the occasional upholstery-stained pimpmobile,
dirty white, convertible, naked lady hood ornament.

My father paces back and forth down the rows,
examining each, opening a hood here, a trunk there,
eyes squinting like an expert's at an auction.
If it was priced under the rolled wad of cash

wedged in his pocket it met his standards and,
of course, if it started, if not immediately, then
after a few solid pumps on the gas pedal, or
if not after a few pumps then with some gas

in the carburetor and a concentrated prayer
that consisted of a deep *shiiiit* to those gods
who controlled the turning over of engines.
He puffs hard on his stub. I screw in the dealer plate:

It's a Terman Motors Special now, he claims,
gunning it, not knowing how long it will run,
or if it can be re-started, or if it will break down
on the way to his used car lot and kill him.

5. The Last of the Hippies

Jesse the bodyman, a pimp on the side, makes the cars hum, in the greasy garage, windowless, tires stacked to the tilting point, country music blasting from the transistor, the toilet backed up, *Playboy* centerfolds shaping the dust, tools haphazard on the cracked cement floor.

"Get you any woman you want," he says, but, seventeen, I sneak phone calls to my girlfriend or lay on the black vinyl couch reading *The Brothers Karamazov,* my father shuffling through car titles on his desk: "Go watch Jesse," he'd say, "You might learn something. Go screw in a plate."

Having to go to the bank, he puts me in charge, shows me a list with two columns scrawled in pencil, one marked "preferred price" and the other "lowest we'll go."

"Back in a few minutes," and no sooner he's out the door, he pauses: "If you get any customers, try to hold them until I get back. Stall them—show them around, start a few cars."

Humid afternoon, air all haze, trash stench from the next door McDonalds, Euclid Avenue screaming, one way downtown, one way the suburbs—my spirit sweating to escape, and Fydor Karamazov murdered just as a customer arrives, all muscle and mirror sunglasses: "I want the Ford in back." My father told me stories about criminals on the lam needing cars in a hurry. He didn't mind: "They always pay up front, cash." As usual, this junker needs a charge-up: the man twitches, Jesse wheels the gigantic battery charger over, cracks the hood, tightens the wires—it juices right up, and I feel the damp of hundreds and fifties; the customer peels out like a drag racer.

My first sale! This long-haired distracted son my father calls *The Last of the Hippies* is worthy and the old man will be proud; he is, he pats me on the back, offers me a cigar, claims in a puff of smoke I'll inherit the business, demonstrates the most important sales tactic: "If a customer looks at a car, don't approach immediately. If he bickers with the price, look him in the eyes and walk away, just walk away," straightening himself by way of demonstration as my customer returns, steaming as the hot sidewalks, blood-faced, pounding his fist on the desk, demanding back his money—he turned the engine off and it won't restart.

My father doesn't look up, cocksure: "Sorry, sir. We sell our cars *as is*." I bury my nose deep into the ravings of Ivan Karamazov to the Grand Inquisitor. "This box here," my father mutters, staring at the form a second too long. "Well, I see it isn't checked," pointing to me: "He sold you the car, didn't he? Well, look at him." Both glare at me as they would a disobedient dog. "He doesn't know nothing."

Later, at home over dinner, my father snips sharply: "How can you be such a *meshugenah*? What do you want to be, anyway?"

"A writer and a teacher."

"I'm glad," he fires back, biting down on his steak as if it was the word and not the piece of meat he was ferociously chewing, "you didn't say: *poet*."

6. A Prayer for Jackie Gleason

The ultimate blue collar,
the man who you had to love
because his story was always

too true. The time, for example,
the mob had him convinced
they were an insurance agency

and hired him to be manager
of their East Side District. We knew
he wanted it all for Alice,

the Cuban cigar,
the apartment on Park Avenue
Ed Norton would envy.

And at the end of each little act
of stupidity, each scam for the life
that would take him away

from the bus he drove
for fourteen years, you had
to forgive him, you just had to,

the way I had to forgive
my father for not paying attention
to the circumstances

of my sadness,
when he'd come home, scrub
his hands as if he could wash

the day out of them, and turn on,
louder than conversation,
The Honeymooners, a re-run he'd seen

so often he'd mouth the words:
to the moon, Alice, to the moon,
Cramden's fat fist punching

his own fat hand,
my father's fat fist
punching his own fat hand.

Last night, long distance,
he'd only say: *Ralph died.*
Sunday afternoons,

we'd drive to look at houses
in wealthier neighborhoods,
Beechwood and Shaker Heights,

but he never closed a deal.
What do I need a new house for?
I got one right here, spreading

the herring soaked in wine sauce
on stale buttered rye bread
and pouring slowly into a coffee cup

a thimbleful of scotch,
JB: *Joe's Booze,* he'd call it,
after himself, so I thought

it was his, and therefore mine.
Slouched against the sink,
he'd gulp it down, then chant,

the way the Great One
wished us goodnight, lips
puckered into a kiss: *Smooothe!*

7. Jokes from the Depression

I was in a hotel room so small
I had to step outside to change
my mind. So dirty a cockroach
handed me the pen to sign in.
Vote for Mo Hair, not Dan Druf.
What time do you go to a Chinese
dentist? Tooth-hurtee.

                    Eventually
they come, one on top of the other
like a sale's pitch, after the table
is cleared, just when I think
I've been spared, this holiday
will be different—this time
we will talk like men
who have pressed the same
wine-colored carpet pacing
from room to room past
familiar furniture, stared
at the same single peach tree
fruitless in the back yard, loved
the same woman in the same house.

Once, in my own apartment,
I looked for a second too long
into the large callused hands
on my desk, had to touch my own face.

Now, my father meets my eyes
over his coffee cup, his face
shadowed with the small hairs
he can never shave away, says

I don't tell my jokes anymore.

I don't tell my jokes any less, either.

And I laugh.

8. A Cast of Thousands

My dad's kid brother, Hy,
worked fourteen-hour days
at Cotton Club Soda Factory
through the Depression and the War,
dreaming of stardom. Eighteen,

wavy black hair, six foot six, dimples,
everyone's head would turn
when he'd stride like an undiscovered star
through the double doors
of Corky and Lenny's Delicatessen

where you would take a number
and order the smoked fish, the lox,
the spicy corned beef, the herring
in wine sauce and sour cream
from the old women in red *shmattes*

speckled with vanilla splotches,
faces patched with rouge and lipstick—
wishing all the customers a *kenina hora*
and filling the air with their *kibbitz* song:
you vant I should slice the challah?

*What's the matter, here you think
it's not fresh?*, in the clatter
and clutter from the meat counter
and the *kvetching* in the corner booth
where the *alter kockers* gathered

and *kibbitzed* about the *machers* and *k'nockers*.
My father had his own parable
about the man who was paid a ruble
per day to wait by the Eastern Wall
for the Messiah: *'How can you work*

for such low wages?' they asked the guy.
Then he said, 'Low wages, sure.
But at least the work is steady.'
His brother, though, hitch-hiked all the way
for a role in *The Ten Commandments*.

He played a slave,
then went into real estate. Each year
it appears around Passover, like Elijah,
and we'd watch close,
my father suddenly pointing to the set:

There he is!
No, wait, there he is!
No, no, I'm sure this time! It's him!,
all of us straining for the familiar face.
He's still the one everybody asks about.

Some days, when it gets dark early,
my father comes home from the used car lot,
kicks the snow off, tells us how none would start
and it seemed his blood would stop
and we should all be in California.

9. Instructions on Climbing Your Father's Garage

At first sign of dark,
climb onto the window ledge—
flatten your hands
on the roof's peeled tar:
all of your body is muscle,
sweat and strain, until
you rise against this
downward stress. Stand
full-length and walk
on the strange surface
twelve feet up, look down
through the basketball net
to the other side. See,
just a few feet beyond,
your father has switched on
the kitchen light: he paces
in and out of your vision,
looking for something, for you.
Turn to the far corner, face
the neighbor's back yard,
sit down, legs dangling
over the edge. Looking into
the millions of stars, count,
until he calls, your blessings.

10. Intensive Care

Pistol cocked against his head,
my father, hand tight in his right pocket,
looks at the customer
who wants the money *and* the car,
and with his left lowers
the automatic delicately
as if it were a broken window shade.

When the bullet tears the flesh,
wrinkled as the cloth I wash cars with,
he feels the powder exploding
from the inside, rising in the lower intestine
until it becomes a taste in the mouth.

At intensive care,
tubes connected to his nose,
he barely lifts his upper-weight toward me, his face
the off-white of the half-dead:

Are you sure
you don't want the lot?
Are you sure?

He is in that place
the anesthesia takes him, floating
around inside forty years
of self-employment.

Each morning means leaning
against the sink, coffee black,
drugged to a day long
with aggravation, the bodyman late,
the ache between customers.

Each night means food on the table,
half dozing on the couch,
face covered with newspaper.

I watch his troubled sleep,
the skin's dark spots,
and know he has willed to me
the labor that is his life.

11. Mourners' Kaddish

1. Terman Motor Sales

Take a long look, I said,
as we left the used car lot
the last day on this earth

I would see my father.
He wanted to take care
of some business before

the surgery, packing
the cars close together
not as if they could, like

flesh, offer each other
warmth in the premature
November freeze, but so that

no one should steal them.
Dirty Cleveland snow layered
over prices chalked clumsily

on windshields, marking them
down to what, my father said,
they were worth. Above:

Terman Motor Sales,
in bright orange and blue paint,
so they can see them from the street,

in the dark. Inside the office
he fiddled with thirty day tags,
finance forms, repossession cards.

Out the window he looked through
for customers, I saw bumpers
of cars, the string of colored pennants,

the traffic, the vacant lots
on the other side. *If I croak,*
I'll haunt all my customers

who owe me money.

2 Sitting Shiva

On hard stools we stare
into snow falling
so thick it's a white-out,

cars motionless, even
in Cleveland, where this
should be a temporary

disturbance. We cover
mirrors with sheets,
pillow cases,

so we aren't reminded
of ourselves,
so that our faces

are plain cloth, thin
coverings, and we return
to each other

and evening
when the house darkens
and we recite the Kaddish,

vis-ga-dal, v'vis'ka
dash, schmay rabo, which
has mention of the loved one,

only of praise and hallowed
be Thy name, only of how
above utterance

is our Redeemer and may
He speedily establish
His Kingdom on earth.

With cracked voices
we pray, swaying
in the name of our loss,

tented like nomads,
wandering Jews, bound
in the bond of our absence.

3. The Tomato Patch

And I imagine the knocking
of his motor click off
after another long day

at the used car lot—
B'olm kir-usey, v-yam lich
mal-chu-say—each of us

with knees bent, bodies
facing the candle, Jerusalem,
in the otherwise dark room,

and, though it is cold
and snowing, in this vision
just outside the window

it is the half-light of August
evening and my father wears
shirt-sleeves, is smoking a cigar—

he kneels into his tomatoes
and examines each one,
tilting and turning, even

the green babies curled
under clumps of leaves,
checks the posts, the soil

for moisture: *May the Lord*
of peace send peace—
he snaps off a red one fat

with juice for the windowsill
above the sink, picks
a few of the not-yet-ripe

for the jars he will seal
with dill, a bay leaf and garlic—
and comfort

the bereaved among us
—hu ya say Shalom—
the seasoning preserved: *Amen.*

12. The Story of Fathers and Sons

My father promised to take me fishing.
I imagined us alone on the rocky pier leaning
into Lake Erie, waiting for sunrise,

him teaching me how to cast and shift
my weight all the way into Canada.
Someday, he said, *someday.*

He lifted his newspaper.
I dreamed of waters.
Now, winds sound like waves

against bare limbs and windows,
crows gather in the dark
and I am far from water or sunrise

or my father sealed in with his blanket
of stars and his book of snow.
What I am fishing for

is my portion of the silence
he passed around the table
like the bread and soup

after the long hard day
and before the long sleepless night—
my anger for the words he broke:

still moments as the tide
smoothed over stones when stories
I'd imagined about fathers and sons

could be true, our eyes skimming
the clean sky in the afternoon quiet—
not for what is exchanged between this

and the other world, but for our shadows
surfacing, for the darker giving out
to the lighter blue water.

He said the journey to the new world
was harder than the trip to the moon.
Astronauts knew there was something solid.

Explorers risked disappearing over the edge.
We looked at the horizon, searched
at the same time for the still point—

and I who have no child and therefore
no promise stare now into tunnels of snow
swirling like white dust and consider

how our words stain the air
with what after all is uncertain
and our desire to make them good.

13. This Lament

Because I do not know the precise moment
when you passed from this world to the next,
or what thought you were in the middle of
that carried you forward into your other life,

what final sound or smell or vision
offered up the earth's message of *farewell,*
and because you took with you the last
expression of your ultimate knowledge,

your heart beating on the other side of silence,
your breath rising and falling in that dimension
that is now more acquainted with you than we are,
that is more familiar with your enormous stature

than those of us who are what you made—
the blood of your blood and the flesh
of your flesh, than we who continue your name
out into the world and claim it as our own,

I cannot know if it resembled the dried stubble
of the winter field emerging gradually
then disappearing into the afternoon mist.
Or was it like a breakdown in traffic, suddenly stalled?

Or was it more the way yesterday's news
I crumple in my fist and place in the wood stove
will all-at-once burst forth into a flame
before transforming into its afterlife of ashes?

Or was it more the way certain words move
from one soul to another, how we carry them
that way, how your transport into what
we can only understand as your Nothingness

has re-emerged into this awkward lament,
the way the stale bread and eggshells
and coffee grounds we dump
into the compost are broken down into soil?

But isn't that my own grief speaking?
A chant or formula that I would want to repeat
to call you back to our known world
as you recede deeper into the airy reaches?

Because I do not know, when you stole away
into the eternal, if it was solitary like the single
yellow primrose on this side of the icy window,
or if you gathered with some new tribe

the way these six white narcissi are bundled
together in a blue vase in the center
of the oak table—if it was rupture or rapture—
if the membrane you passed through

was translucent like these blurred mourning doves
caught up in the fog or whether it had the clarity
of washed glass a swallow will collide against,
or if it was more like the lover's skin we smooth

our tongues along in our serious investigations,
seeking out the scars and bumps and bruises
and tiny hairs of our ecstasies, I cannot know
if that narrow room where you left us

was the same room that received you
with its silent applause, the way, when we love,
the pine-board ceiling and the swirling dust,
the lint glistening in the carpet, the candlelight

flickering and now doubled in the new dark,
take on the quality of a deeper
suffusion, and we are suddenly unstable
as water, weightless and floating.

Coda: My Father Calls My Name in the Voice of a Bird

A bird I can't identify
cries from the next field
its two notes: *Phil-up,*

Phil-up, the way my father
would caterwaul my name
up the stairs for supper.

I still hear him, though
from the other world,
clamor for me to gather

in the feasting. If so,
it would be Sunday night
and steak medium rare,

sautéed with onions,
fried potatoes on the side.
It was his meal

and as far of heaven
as in his life he'd believe.
He taught us to suck the meat

clean of the bone.
But what if these echoes
have nothing to do

with my father and me?
What if the bird is exclaiming
its own hunger from the spruce

and, as is most likely, sounds
like a familiar voice only because
I want, like everyone,

for my beloved dead to live again?

Two:

Attachments

Home Movie: The Bris

In thirty-eight year old static,
on the screen torn at the edges,
my relatives again gather
around the living room table,
some familiar, some I reconstruct
out of dimly recalled
stories. They all hunch
toward the center, the men
wearing yarmulkes, the women shawled.
Two strangers stand aside
to reveal the eight-day infant,
myself, born of this house
and lying face up on the white
sheet, palms grasping for a mother's
absent hands. It is all black and white.
I squirm and cross my legs
as I watch the *mohel* wash
the thin blade in the glass
bowl of holy water, wipe it
against the towel my father,
young as I am now, holds,
that soon will be stained
with blood. Fixing the knife
in the air, a few inches above
the chilled flesh, the *mohel* mouths
the words from the gold-plated
Book: *This is my covenant,*
which ye shall keep, between me
and thee, and thy seed after thee,
the blade slowly caressing
the private part of the shadowed

body, and in the blur
of spliced film, he slices
around the penis, the foreskin
thin as an insect's wing. Now,
everybody shakes hands—*l'chiams,*
mazel tovs without sound—
as I feel once more my heart
beating behind its outward flesh.

The Shvitz

If the *Torah* is our lives,
our portion was sung in that sanctuary
of a steamhouse by a *minyan* of ten
thirteen-year-old boys and a counselor,
a secular rabbi who knew the streets
like an emissary from the world
where our lives are already sealed.

He led us past the sign that still reads
members only, listed in the phone book
as *The Russian Bath and Tea Room,*
but known to the initiates as *Sweat*
in Yiddish, on 116th and Luke, our parents'
old neighborhood when all the world
was kosher and on Sabbath mornings

they walked in tennis shoes under
laundry drying above the street,
past houses of uneven boards
and sunken roofs, the fishmarket,
the famous Zeiger's Delicatessen,
before it changed, all except this small
brownstone, with a *mezuzah* on the door.

In front of the lockers I imitated his motions
as he took off his suit coat, muscles bulging
behind white shirt and tie, his pants,
the undershirt, the underwear, and I was afraid
to go on, to show myself in front of strangers.
Come on, he said, *here we're all the same,*
underneath. Once, late at night,

just we two gave each other backrubs
on his living room floor. My shoulder blades
felt like wings beneath his moist palms
as he rubbed down my back and around
the inside of my arms, kneading
my flushed skin with his fingertips.
I was one body touching another body.

Here, cots with clean sheets lined
the central room. He instructed: *After
we sweat, we rest*. Adjacent, the dining area:
kosher pickles and hot peppers in bowls
under a photograph of the Wailing Wall:
After we rest, we eat. Steaks with garlic
broiled in the stove: *Then we go sweat some more*.

We were with history.
But all we knew was that we were naked
among men who were reading newspapers
or talking about how it was all changing
and the law was in our own hands.
Our counselor led us into the steamroom
where old men sat on towels beside buckets

of cold water they'd pour over their heads
and fill up again. We began at the lower
bench, facing the hole in the wall where
the sandstones glowed like burning bushes,
then moved up, rising with the heat, daring
the others to lie full length at the top,
long as they could stand it, longer,

until the room was so full of gray mist
we became outlines of figures floating
in a secluded heaven, simmering out
all of our small tensions, and still he'd say:
Throw in more water, it's not hot enough—
our heads down, my hands, like his, gripping
splintered wood against the oncoming rush.

Eloquence

"...for I am slow of speech, and of a slow tongue."
—Moses to God

Born defective, roof of mouth
too splintered, a cracked
bowl, pallet cleft like
tabernacles and so my speech
is impeded, my *S's* slurred,
my *R's* never rounded out,
and I know to repeat myself
like a foreigner, as if my first
was my second language.
Kids made their usual fun: *Listen*
to the one with the bone
in his mouth. In speech class,
I resisted reshaping the figures
my tongue made in the shelled
spaces of the cheeks, the air
between teeth, quivering upward
like a needle in its compass,
into the deep gulf of the North,
where I exiled unsaid syllables,
at home in their deformed privacy,
the way, I learned, the tongue of Moses
clung to its dome. Pharaoh
gave him a choice of gold or live coals.
No god, Moses reached for the coins,
but the angel descended to push
and fold his fingers over what
was torn out of the earth
and on fire, charring the flesh Moses

quickly pressed to his lips,
scorching his tongue, a small bush
burning. His brother was his voice,
his mouthpiece before the people,
but when he conversed with the silence,
as I write on this page, he wandered
off by himself and spoke alone.

Yom Kippur

We swallow our own spit.
From sundown to sundown,
the ache in the stomach
is a small spot expanding
until it holds all of them,
a year's worth: *for the sins
we have committed against Thee
without thought, for the sins
we have committed against Thee
knowingly.* Once a year
we walk away from our labor,
the soft autumn light filtering
through emptying trees, to fill
the sanctuary with atonement.
The rabbi is a black speck
in this House of God
as he recites from scrolls lit
by the light that burns everlasting.
We read our errors responsively,
a congregation of wrongs,
billions of dead voices chanting
through our mouths, our fingers
quivering from right to left
under the strange black letters
read by our parents and their parents
before them, every lunar turning
the same words, until, finally,
we will get them right, and the dome
that covers our heads like a white
skullcap opens and light erases
the parchment and no one will

have to read them again, no one,
all our stupid sins singed
away like pieces of flesh
stripped from their skeletons,
our lives slowly becoming
strange to us, as we arrive,
gaunt, ravished, to break the fast.

My Father's Mother

There she is with my father,
the only portrait of the two of them,
holding each other, perhaps dancing.

My father is a grown man already,
handsome in black suit, before
he gained the weight, lost the hair.

She's smiling but old, having birthed
six children, her husband in a wheelchair,
moving from place to place to place

and that's all I know about her,
except her name, beginning with a *P*,
same as mine, no coincidence,

I'm her namesake, the next child born,
her replacement. My father never spoke of her,
only that they were poor, and maybe

that's why, or maybe he thought
I wouldn't be interested in the dead,
or maybe the past is too many griefs,

which are our real ancestors after all,
our chromosomes are filled with them,
that look and smile like us, answer

to our names. But we long for a hairpin,
a shawl stained with overuse and mold,
a letter, a torn phrase in her hand: *Yussel,*

please, will you pick me up a little milk?,
so from this scanty evidence we can note
the details and make up the rest:

Cleveland, 73rd and Templett, first floor
apartment, she's breastfeeding my father,
the last one, her hair undone, shouting,

half-English, half Yiddish, to my grandfather
who yells from the next room for some herring
and whiskey, the infant making teethmarks

in her delicate skin, she will be up all night,
and the Depression—I, too, need her—
to dance, stranger, flesh of my flesh.

Attachments

How they say we should be free of them,
how we can just shut our eyes in silence
and practice forgetfulness, focus on one word
and repeat it over and over until it opens

out like a door into a world full of nothing
or a flower's unfolding, water into water,
the space we arose out of and will descend
back into, the story of the child who approaches

with the lighted torch. When I asked
Where does the flame come from?, he blew it out
and asked me in turn: *Where has it gone?*
A hinge creaking into the other world,

where our life and death aren't, an unfamiliar
voice, a stained letter, the moment I lift
my eyes into the hummingbird's flight,
or toward my grandfather's ancient scale

he'd measure the fruit with then peddle down
the narrow red-brick streets of Cleveland's
Jewish section, its black numbers fainted
through scratched glass, the frayed rope

holding the container that cradled apples
and bananas and grapes and oranges—
It's a living, he'd say, and now it hangs
in the kitchen window, holding an African violet,

its purple flowers shimmering in diffused light
that, they say, after seeking into your original
nature, will reveal enlightenment, when
the bottom of the pail is broken through.

It's a living, he'd repeat, hauling the fruit
in his horse and wagon and soon he was
in the junk business. He wore his hat,
like Whitman, inside and out. He ate

mustard from the jar. He just missed the Titanic.
How if we sit in a certain position and allow
our thoughts to follow like streams their natural directions...
If we understand the inner-workings of the wheel...

When he was six, in the Pale of Russia, where
because of his birth and belief he was exiled,
he was wrapped in a prayer shawl and presented
to the synagogue so he could become intimate

with the Holy of Holies. All his life an acquaintance
with the Eternal so when he went from one junkyard
to another he could in his mind chant any of the 613
commandments and perhaps the One

whose name could not be spoken but to whom
he could always speak would be listening. The scale
is holding still and balanced, the way he would cup me
in his stubby and scarred hands. Nathan.

He died soon after. I never knew him in the way
we mean the word, so this workaday object,
this work of art, with the fainted words *tested* and *sealed*
and *Ohio,* is all I have of his outward life,

his living my inheritance. How they say
what you are seeing is only form. I want to stare
at this round numbered circle and see a face
wrinkling over itself as in water, mine, my mother's, his.

My Life as a Child

The leaves of that willow
are wet with light. October afternoon,
3 p.m., the hour when the school bus stops
on corners like Scrubgrass and Mill

and they fly out like tiny birds twitching
from your cupped hands and soar
their way home through air so clear
and still it is held breath or an empty

bottle or a dream remembered whole.
Heartbreaking, you said, these glazed
white farmhouses, this road winding
like mist over a river, this woman

who gave us directions. She's gathered
weeds and branches from the surface
of the water, establishing rhythms,
setting the ripples back in motion,

wheeling her compost
back to its source. This morning
happened cold and beautiful, sun
spreading its ocher net through

the cornstalks and around the orchard:
the king apple, apple of abundance,
the light taking its time surfacing
until it scrubwashed the sky over

Scrubgrass Road. I walked
into the woods under white oak,
black oak, chokecherry, thornapple,
maple, quivering ash, and stood under

the famous poplar and stared up
its slender spine that rises and branches out
like a rabbi's benediction signifying the end
of something, or its beginning, these

Holy Days, these Days of Awe, between
the sounding of the *shofar*
with its one hundred blasts thundering
through the deep hollows of the synagogue

and the thinning down of the body, like death,
between when our names are inscribed
in the Book or not and when they are
for another year sealed. *Heartbreaking,*

this solitude and silence, this late-afternoon-
into-evening-reverence, these yellow-red
leaves of that front-yard tree, the glassy air,
the solemn hour, this open porch,

this stained oak porchswing
and bean soup simmering on the dark side
of the screen door. In the memory
of my life as a child I am always seven.

Once, after the bell, I ran full-speed
down the suburban street—it was
just this light pouring down, those certain
moments between school and supper,

and I knew how much living
it would take to die: broken bones,
long illness, skin cut and opened, unfilled years.
I was a few inches above the sidewalk.

I looked into the distance: *This is where I am.*
We lost one once. It was no larger
than a star seen from the earth,
placed on the bathroom sink in its red tissue:

placenta, body, spine, the miniature human
shape visible by flashlight, no head, no breath.
We stared at it, what we made. We carried it into the darkness
in tissue paper like some kind of gift

and gave it back to the earth.
Beside the back porch, the compost pit,
under my grandmother's mint which came
from another world, like her creased hands,

her Yiddish tongue.
We said: *Hear, Oh Israel.*
It was what this moment will become:
October dusk, the moon a sliver from full.

It had no name, as if it were perfect.
Only a blood relation can stand and recite
in the synagogue the words of the mourners.
But on the Day of Atonement everyone alive grieves for
  everyone dead.

Around our solitude and silence we want
someone we love to plant roses. Now
the circular moon forms its silver outline
out of the sky's autumnal consummation,

a perfection, we agree, we believe in, pure
as the man-without-child standing
in a field of full afternoon light that is already
a memory or the moment just before loneliness,

or when we rise to the next, which is the last, world.

The Synagogue in Oil City, Pennsylvania

The congregation disappears one by one
into another service underground or on top
of the air where there is no trouble

making a *minyan* like there is here
in this temple above the Allegheny River
and a block from where, less and less,

tankers rattle over the Petroleum Bridge,
carrying their crude. Orthodox,
not allowed to use the phone on this day

of rest, have Frank, the gentile neighbor
with the orange hunting jacket, call up
any Jews still left because you need

at least ten so that each prays
for the entire and not only for the self.
During the Torah portion no longer

the sound of drills, the derricks pumping,
but now the quiet grows with each responsive
chanting, each loss making a little more room

to be filled in by a mysterious God.
The names on the scroll of the dead outnumber
the names called to read from the Book

or carry it on their shoulders around
the tabernacle, singing in the Sabbath.
So many injunctions to lift over their bodies.

The children left with the economy
and will not return. These are the last
generation in a town with no rabbi,

who took a better job. And who can blame him,
not wanting to be the one to bury them all,
these final chosen to keep the word here,

where they gather out of habit or a faint
calling in the blood like those birds
who return to the same place the same time

to sing together in their sanctuary
until it is filled, like this town
after the refinery closes, with silence.

The Wounds

Our wounds are according to instructions.

The recipe calls for one scar each, a searing
of our sex, a cut where it would most hurt,
our lives starting with a scream, a loss,
pieces of skin we pay with in advance.

If it's our blood we bequeath,
will we live lives of holiness?

Will we be rewarded for our severings?

Will we be called out of the congregation
to open the curtains of Your Book?

Will we carry it on our shoulders
around the synagogue on the Days of Awe?

What will You do with these wicks, these tips
of grass, these flecks of light?

Will You write on our accumulated flesh
the words You did not say concerning Auschwitz?

What We Pass On

I was a Bilfield, she begins,
starting with the name her father
gave her, *before I was a Terman.*

She is sitting at the kitchen table,
facing the clock with the Hebrew letters,
its poorly tuned motor a perpetual moan

in the background when the house
is full, louder when she's alone
among furniture and portraits.

The names of Jews, she says, *were for
their occupation, what they did.
A "feld" meant a large field. My grandparents*

*worked in a large field, green,
wildflowers, in summer. Austria-
Hungary. The shtetl I'm not sure of.*

I have it written down somewhere.
What happened to that name: Bilfield,
field? My mother keeps it tucked

between other names. Whenever
I do anything right—get up early,
set the table before she comes home—

I'm a Bilfield, a field with yellow
and blue and white, a meadow
in a country no longer there,

divided and portioned out like
its people scattered under the grass
or in other lands, their names diminished,

their language attenuating to hushes,
breaths stuttered into the ears
of children—phrases from a Yiddish

they strain to hear, like the story she tells now
about her grandparents Shmu-el
and Malka. Their portraits hang on the wall:

Shmu-el: gray streaks in a beard
that bunches past his white collar,
the black coat of the peasant

and the black square hat
because wherever he was
he was in the House of God.

His eyes stare into the future
as if it were an obligation.
And the other, Malka, for whom

my mother was named:
Malka, Mildred—
the first letter of the most recent dead

passes on, the rest of the name
we fill in for ourselves—so what
is left of us is an initial, one capital

letter, a sound signifying human
to remind us that we are spelled out
of those who came before—

Malka, sad faced, babushka
wrapped around thin hair, looped
across tired breasts, the forehead

wrinkled and around the eyes
marks of claws, pupils staring
in slightly different directions,

the right tilted upwards signaling
worship, the left off to the side
signaling caution and there's something—

these figures, inside their original frames,
sketched in pencil and charcoal,
dusted with one-hundred-year-old light,

something, not in the noses or chins,
the mouths fixed as if the barest smile,
a grin, would be an effort—but something

in my mother's voice: *Shmu-el*
was an Elder—I have it written down
somewhere—and the Germans

lined him up and they shot him
and Malka came across with a son
they discovered to be tubercular

so the officials at Ellis Island
wouldn't let him in. Imagine—
she left these portraits with a relative

and made the long journey back
so the son shouldn't make the trip alone,
coughing up blood, both disappearing

on the other side of the waters
in the country of hardship, but where—
we can only guess. My mother's eyes

turn and lock into mine: *Yes—*
her head nods to the rhythm
of the clock moaning: *we can guess.*

Three:

Houses

In the Ridiculous Hour

of 4 a.m., under the pale stars, I walked beyond
the sleeping houses toward the cemetery,
followed the circular gravel path around
the gravestones, as if I were the rabbi
and they the obscure congregation.
I gathered them together in a sanctuary.
We recited responsively the prayer for the dead,
not the way it's done in a synagogue service,
where only the ones whose grief is recent
are required to raise their workaday bones
and chant and sway under the majestic dome,
but rather I told them they could remain
where they were, to assume their relaxed position.
They need not turn to the proper page
in the prayer book or even pay attention.
Though the hour was illegible, I sanctioned
each stone—the steady and the leaning,
those placed in a constellation
and those settled off in a plot by themselves,
to acknowledge after me: *once,*
that's all we live, a religion in a moment.
The gold crescent moon was holding
the new moon in its arms, coyotes howling
their distinct rhythms in the nearby distance.
Each body has forsaken its rumbling fire
and chosen to appear here, in this afterlife of light.
I invented a ritual that interwove them
with the stars in one benediction. Who can say
it won't evolve one day into a tradition?
I sermonized in silence. It was a commentary
on our entire testament. It felt like a Sabbath,

the way the air was held, preserved, as if in a jar
and left undisturbed from the world.
I don't know how I could be so observant
and still miss the thin ocher light at the horizon,
and the stars were gone—once, once, once.
And the names slowly emerged out of their dark closets.

From the Heartland

The pear tree in my backyard
is bursting its green fruit. All day
the breeze quivers the lilacs and the sky
is so vast one person can't take it all in,
the cornfields and farms stretched
beyond the reach of my single vision.

The other day I finally saw a heron.
A friend and I were hiking the Skunk,
winding the curves, the river allowing us
the marsh and foxtails and black-eyed Susans
and there she stood: austere, gray feathers
giving solidity to the mist,

contained in solitude, inhabiting
the same silence we were staring into.
Why she spun to give air to her wonder
is beyond me, or why she remained
to swirl in a circle, a confirmation
of feathers, silvered in the spray,

and the rippled screech, I can only guess at. And
the deliberate raising of the wings,
just before the soaring.
This is the heartland, love,
the midst of somewhere, the place
where the constant crying of the trains

is lives passing through you.
They would be your music,
if you sat on the porch and read until
the pages darkened and the smell of your lover
cooking fresh mushrooms and rice brought you inside.
At night, in this town they call *Ames,*

in this county they call *Story,*
the stars are visible from any road,
reassuring you the sky is in place.
The streets are tree-lined
and the houses have spaces all to themselves,
bicycles on lawns, kids on skateboards in driveways.

In curtain-drawn windows you can see
relatives on wooden chairs sitting in a circle,
trying to get everyone into the talk.
What talk?
No more about the brown corn, the sadness
of the Midwest, only that the nights are cooler

and thank god for school and it doesn't matter
what anyone says, they met the candidates
and can make up their own minds. What they have
is a sky so wide they claim distance
for themselves, the land and the neighbors
surrounding, far as the horizon will allow.

Without Closure

...it was like that trail we hiked at Yellowstone,
the one that never looped back around.
We followed orange markers, jingling keys

to scare off bears, past burned-out trees,
limbs blackened from the last summer's blaze.
Everywhere fireweed sprouting after the forest flames,

something about the way carbon mixes with air,
something scientific, but I saw it as a metaphor
for how their few inches of stalky purple beauty

relied on the destruction of thousands of years.
She picked one, curled it behind an ear, and we walked,
across a stream, through a field, though we heard

distant thunder and the sky folded like the countless
corridors of a hawk's wing. And then the hail: white
stones, biblical, driving us into the trees, the wind

picking up and cooling down, our skin chilled,
her face buried in my chest: *It can't last long,*
I whispered, but I imagined the rangers reading

our names in the large black book we'd signed,
searching for bodies, newlyweds, unprepared
for the sudden changes in mountain weather,

without raingear or compass to find ourselves
or even the knowledge of just how cold and lost
the other could be without completely breaking down.

I want to write to her while she's still alive
and I can speak into her ear in a clear voice
words I have cultivated through the narrow prism

of countless sleepless nights. We loved.
We worshipped wild in our house of prayer.
We spoke of how the future transformed the past

and were silent as I slid the ice over her bare skin
in the hottest part of the summer. Trees stood still,
curtains, curves of legs, arms, neck, brown,

the slow motion seizure of the Midwest afternoon.
We were married and could do anything we wanted
with desire and each other. We washed dishes.

We said blessings. We drove madly across the country.
I laid my head on her lap one October in a town
in Wisconsin and the sun slanted squinting my eyes.

She sang me to sleep and I woke inside her,
to the new dark, to everything unfamiliar,
as if we were following some higher law,

distinct in the taste of apples she'd saved,
behind the art museum, holding each other's face
in the foreknowledge of our bereavements.

Now the night is splitting into pieces
of memory and I'm trying to fix our moments
the way I try to identify lights in the sky

as either planets or stars, but they are impossible
to detail like the confusion I tried to walk off
those evenings after supper toward a cornfield

distance, the houses small and serious, ours among them,
with gardens and a clear view of the enormous
summer that cut through our rooms—

something about wanting or not wanting a child,
and how our stories of the future became open-ended.
What is certain floats like a parachute and lands

in a tree with canvas and ropes all over itself.
Now I live alone in a small quiet town by a river
and imagine her doing the same, busy in her life

and filled with the glory of this fall,
the yellow and red leaves glittering in after-rain,
like the stars that shine so long after their passing.

Some Days

Some days you have to turn off the news
and listen to the bird or the truck
or the neighbor screaming out her life.
You have to close all the books and open
all the windows so that whatever swirls
inside can leave and whatever flutters
against the glass can enter. Some days
you have to unplug the phone and step
out to the porch and rock all afternoon
and allow the sun to tell you what to do.
The whole day has to lie ahead of you
like railroad tracks that drift off into gravel.
Some days you have to walk down the wooden
staircase through the evening fog to the river,
where the peach roses are closing,
sit on its grassy bank and wait for the two geese.

Meditation in Oil City, Pennsylvania

The windows of Electralloy Steel
glare out at the black river

meaning the workers are punched in
and the sky will greet travelers

driving in on Route 8 out of Franklin
with handfuls of smoke rising

like gray balloons to the stars
we can no longer see or name.

When the young oil executive
out of New York moved in with his wife

she smelled the greasy air,
broke down, and cried. But

on a Sunday night, the snow sparkling
like silver coins above the empty blocks,

lights off in the living rooms, you can almost
believe again in the old magical formula

of how oil equals money equals Victorian
mansions equals comfort. The derricks

and other creatures not found in nature
have disappeared into the imaginations

of dead capitalists. All the trees
have shed their soot, the railroad

has rolled up its rails for the night,
and we are all working hard in the dark,

dreaming of wind blowing away smoke,
of Orion letting down his sword and belt.

Oil City Serenade

Let's walk down to the Petroleum Bridge,
where the Allegheny cuts the town in half,
shielded from the sharp beams of Route 8
that glow like searchlights now that dusk
seeps beyond the hills steep as walls
pushing against boarded-up buildings
and dead-end streets. Smell grease
in the air, chemicals that float like wounded
birds from the one refinery left, and
if that goes, they say, we're done. Tonight,
a dozen teenage boys cruise West First Street
and catcall the almost women smoking
in front of the video store, all that's open
and no school tomorrow, these bodies of time
and desire fused in by the hills and bends,
a sky too far away to be believed.
Blackbirds call and gather and fill branches
with signals and silence. Let's cross
the rusted rails, our way lit by the Dipper
forming a large question mark. We'll simply
look at the water, a clear black,
its surface reflecting the freeway's flames
that flicker from the great candelabrum
of the underworld. Earlier, we walked the streets,
not unnamed but unmarked, past the sunken
porches, the for-sale signs, upward and upward
into where the money lived. We gazed
at the mansions of the oil men, the garrets
and the spires, their reward for turning this
all into cash, every fifth one for sale.

Tires shriek, high-pitched screams, the air explodes
with the future. Take out a coin. Toss it into the current
and wish—a slight splash and then the sinking.

If We Were as Brilliant as Groundhogs

We know these are the shortest days:
late dark, early dark, we've adjusted
in our own fashions to the degrees
of gray, maneuvering down icy roads

to spend hours in dusty rooms reciting
the literature of our complaints. But now
the clouds have decided to disperse
and the pre-dawn moon re-appears,

having experimented with how long
we could live without it, like a lover
vanishing into an inexplicable privacy,
or a God who needs the reassurance

that we are unable to live without Him.
Yes, that's what the light is for us:
we can take its absence only so far.
At first we rejoiced in its leave-taking,

its daily requirements of radiance, glarings
and exposures, its requisite pleasures,
the burden of beauty's full view, content
to bear what our new lives require:

turning inward, taking deliberate steps,
the deeper silences, sudden distances,
mist gathering and receding, monochrome
and framed, objects blurring into themselves:

trees into sky, water into field, the sudden
bursts of snowfall from the place the stars were.
And the flashflames of the smaller gods
who carry what remains of light: blue jay

and cardinal, red-headed woodpecker,
red-streaked finch, enough to keep most
happy, reminders of what once was
and harbingers of what will come again.

But for others it's not enough—a flick
of an occasional flight is only a gesture,
some cosmic mockery meant to tease
or test their resolve for just how much

they can stand, stuck in their houses,
relying on their own inner resources.
If we were as brilliant as groundhogs
we'd sleep through it, sink deeply

into the muddy caves of our own bodies
and dream the dream of the inactive,
practicing for our own deaths, suspending
almost completely our blood, like the waters

of this immediate earth, until the stirring,
as now, the prodigal light roaring across
the horizon, blinding us in its harsh return,
daring us once again back into our own lives.

Meditation in Winter

I always wanted to know what rain
turning into snow looked like, its light
huddling inside small black ponds

like children most alive and in secret,
each moment a further transformation
into their own particular angels.

We pile more wood into the stove fire
as geese sound from gray invisibility
their farewells and a red-headed woodpecker

pierces one at a time the pieces of bread
and now a mourning dove and now
a junco touch into the waiting room

of tall grasses and dried leaves,
pecking, impatient, the way their wings
bide time in each feather cell

for their natural region of the air.
The junco has crawled inside
the plastic cage of the feeder and is

half-buried in grain and seeds,
perched in its desire, absorbed
in the lucky greed of its life,

in what binds it back to its earth
and sets it once again soaring—
in the middle distance the spruce trees,

in the further distance the arborvitaes
holding their share of soil and green,
like resolutions, and everywhere

the snow flaking from a greater abundance.

Swallows

We discovered them by accident,
in the complicated
architecture of their nest,
a bristled upside down
skullcap or crown of thorns,
fixed as if permanently
to the rafter in a shadowed
corner of the barn
like a sculpture in bas-relief—
mud and straw
and twigs and doghair—
more secured to their board
than the hardwood itself
is to the beam. Inside,
four, just-hatched and tiny
as our pinkies' finger-
nails, still clinging
to bits of their broken shells,
down moist from the other world.
In a Soho gallery
it would be called naive
and prominently featured
in a showcase labeled:
Artist unknown. Materials:
Northwest Pennsylvania,
tagged well beyond
the means of the middle class.
Each day between rototilling
and fixing the lawn tractor
and looking for the proper hoe
we would stand tiptoe

on the mud floor and peer
into their private place.
They'd curl around each other
into a center like one
pulsing animal. Counting
each additional feather
we noticed the stubs
of wingbones and knew
they would soon be gone.
We had to call them fledglings,
stacked like ornaments one
on top of the other, framed
against the sliver of June sky
visible through the slats,
staring up at us with eyes
black as dark wells.
Their mother allowed
those few moments of silence
before squawking us away.
In dusk they one by one
flew straight at us,
their transgressors, into our emptiness.

In This Hour of Privacy

Invisible birds,
sing your songs of sweet emptiness.

Weave through the blue light
the language of the other world.

Pine cones,
fall one at a time and rest in the shadows.

Answer the occasional cow bellows from distant pastures.

Wind, embrace
the lilacs and blueberry bushes
in their stony stillness, the apple trees
in their humid terrors, the white flowers

of the mock orange that will explode
their revelations.

Compel us into a silence and a fevered straining.

We are on the edge of time,
on the fractured blade of death.

We are no longer living as we once were.

As we listen we imitate
the rosebuds in their bursting.

We are as blurred as this light,
as frail as water, and as afraid, and as helpful.

Shave the hair off your body,
sing the frogs from the eye of the pond,
despite the injunction to let it grow even in the afterlife.

We make ourselves as bare as the grass, as the stars,

follow the suggestion of a rhythm,
branches in an uncertain breeze,
our skin's urging toward a phenomenal dusk.

Saying a cadence, our breath is a labor and a compulsion.

And in this hour of privacy,
shall we know the mourning dove's flight
out of the spruce tree?

Note the incomplete nest,
placed near an open window like an unfinished book,
its twigs and deer hair wreathed like the unkempt crown
     of Jesus
in the painting where his eyes are dark wells.

Rise like so many rustlings,
like slow fires accounted for by the ancients.

Say farewell to the earth for awhile.

Saturday Night Blues Hour

We wear loose clothes,
dancing in the kitchen
to the antique radio

with its bent antenna directed
toward the appropriate star—
Sabbath evening slow blues hour,

from Pittsburgh, simmering
with the chicken, onions, garlic,
what the scholars, who should know,

having considered the matter
for centuries, say is a foretaste
of perfection. All week we've stacked

hay against the house, gathered apples,
put to bed the garden, filled the feeders.
Tonight we eat an extra meal

and grow another soul
for the other world,
which requires our presence

in the cardinal's flight
out of the sweetgum tree and in each unfolding
of sky and in our clumsy waltzing

to John Lee and Muddy and Koko
moments before sundown as our departed
ancestors drape us in their holy dark.

Isaiah at Rest

All day I've been reading Isaiah,
who I imagine to be ordinary,
in love with a woman who like you

grows and then cooks the vegetables
and only cares about a happy life.
Ye shall be confounded for the gardens

that ye have chosen doesn't apply to her,
he meant it in a more rhetorical way.
And when he arrives home late, his voice

gone, his throat aching, feet scarred
and scratched from all the hard roads,
she puts in front of him a bowl

of last season's harvest: potatoes, tomatoes,
carrots, onions, basil, fennel, dill.
It tastes in his mouth not *as the tongue*

of fire devours the stubble
or *as the dry grasses sinketh down in the flame*
but more flavorful of their earth

than the live coals that touched his lips
and took away his iniquities. He loosens
the girdle of righteousness from his waist,

and takes off completely the girdle
of faithfulness from his loins,
being in any case more full

of the knowledge of his sources.
All flesh is grass, he whispers
into her ear and the smell

of his fiery breath
makes her ask him to whisper it
again.

For Ganya

Hebrew for garden. The wise say to take another name
and hide it from everyone so that God can call us
in the night. You chose yours out of your calling.
Scrubgrass Road, Venango County, Pennsylvania,
across from the Amity Church and its cemetery,
where the road rises and gives the land its southern slope,
so what grows will be first to bud and last to frost.

Out of your life study, your real work, your daily art,
waking and sleeping, your thoughts and blood attending
to each season, rising in first light, resting with the dark,
daylight animal, dream animal. Off Old Route 8,
between Clintonville and Mercer, Grove City and Franklin,
what the rural postal carrier calls *The Lord's Protected*.
Under the same slate commissioned to roof

this red brick one-room schoolhouse, *1884* carved
above the entrance, dating our dwelling the way
the mezuzah, slightly tilted, nailed to the maple doorpost,
is a reminder to teach words scripted from time's
other side and to speak of them and to bind them
as a sign and to wear them as frontlets
on the forehead the way birds are distinctively marked,

like these winter survivors lighting around the birdfeeder:
the fluffed-up blue jay perched on the twisted blueberry bush,
the cardinal's occasional flame-flash, the surprise feather-
whistle of the mourning dove, its sleek neck jerking
at groundseeds, the woodpecker davening on the sycamore,
the omnipresence of the chickadees, the common juncos,
the snowbird hovering where wheatfield edges into wood

in the winged pages of a bedside book. From stiff leaves,
spruce cones, lopsided apples, hardened with the season.
From dried-out sunflower seeds whose stalks
only months ago were taller than our heads, taller
than the telephone wires, leaves large as tabletops,
from popcorn husks clothespinned to the greenhouse rope,
from canning and preserving, from consuming the past

in the present, from mint we transplanted from beside my
   Russian
grandmother's rented wrap-around porch: you took this
   name.
From eggshells and coffee grounds and carrot bits
in the compost pit we made with scrap lumber and fence wire.
From skunk cabbages that conceal their flowers in marshes
along the spring that feeds the pond where you showed me
the tadpoles as they one by one broke out of their sacs

and announced themselves to the water: *Ganya,*
from the moody breezes, the meaningful weather, the
   invisible
spirits of the deer who in half-light leave their signatures
and night-huddle in clearings. From raccoon-in-the-corn
   fear,
rabbit fear, chemical-spray-from-neighbors fear. From fresh oak
   floors
and old oak burning off bone chill, its ash we scatter
on the garden snow. From everything becoming everything
   else.

From our previous lives, our deep griefs, our broken
hearts. From our renewed desires, our fierce attractions,
our mating calls and embarrassments, here we are,

magazines piling up in the corner, skullcaps and candles
stored in the cupboard, our property of good silences,
our casual arrangements, our serious talk, in the washed air,
in the fog hovering like a friendly animal among the
    arborvitaes.

From our privacy where we move by touch, allowing
the inner reaches, the bumps and bruises, the curves.
Before the day with its duties, the bells, the talk, the shuffling,
the visible sores. You are sinewy like ironwood, hard bark,
taut, tightened, stretched thin as the flesh over your cheekbones
my fingertips shape in the natural light. Your face is
    luminescent,
a flame illuminating its candle, water shimmering under
    close stars.

Before the gray light and the dust swirls, the scraping of bowls,
the spills, doors closing, the coughs and the news of bombs,
I massage your inner thighs, my tongue circling your small
    hairs.
Before the alarm, before the cold porcelain, the traffic
and the necessary anxieties, you open up your body and I enter.
Once, a robin beat on the window, saying there was vastness
    here.
Wings against glass said we could offer it further flight.

Once, another chirped in the chimney, chiding,
joining our conversation. But it was fear speaking,
out of the spine of the house. You opened the ash door:
orange-reddish breast and throat, streaked with black,
olive eyes spotted as the coarse grass and reeds and mud
it nests in. You grabbed hold of its feathers, its pulsing belly
against your pulsing palms, flung it back into its distance.

The dead students know we keep the schoolhouse unlocked.
They gather here as if still assigned. They recall days
when it was one great room to reassure themselves
that the angel of knowledge, for whom these bricks
were fired a half-mile away, carted in wheelbarrows,
stacked and mortared and pointed to last
centuries, the labor of learning, still latinizes here.

The story goes that the builder Robert Sterret called it
Victory Two because his wife wanted it someplace else:
the second time he ever got his way with her.
Leonard Riddle, the student badboy, told us this,
in his middle-of-the-pasture trailer the other side of Mill Road.
He chewed so much tobacco he had permanent lines
of dried-up juice stained on either side of his chin.

Cold mornings, he said, the teacher was the first to arrive
and lit the pot-bellied stove. Some of the boys
would get there earlier, stuff corn stalks down the chimney
for a day off. Said sixty years ago there weren't many trees.
You'd be five miles away and, after a day of wood gathering,
splitting, hauling, stacking, you'd gaze over the acres
at the schoolhouse and the church: always in view,

learning and God and knowing-what's-ahead
like spring's arrival, each year, as recorded in the First Book.
The genesis of coltsfoot, daffodils, the irises
and the columbines. The struggle for the rare flower,
the trillium, secret all year but for its subtle passage.
Shaped in threes: leaflets, sepals, petals of its solitary star,
red or white, its only knowledge the knowledge of early
   spring.

We strained our eyes for it, brief rumor.
We risked our lives in the crevices, balancing ledges.
We examined the earth with our countless leanings,
among boulder and spring, slag chips and hidden lovers.
It wasn't until we gave up that it was revealed, in the marsh.
We lay in the damp and floated in its lily-herbs.
We licked hidden places, lolling in swampy love.

You said the garden is earned one spadeful at a time:
onions, thin as hairpins, germinating in flats and cellpacks,
barely visible under the grow lights: pumpkin rouge,
butternut squash, cucumbers, melons, lettuces, cabbage,
too-numerous-to-list tomatoes, peppers from pimiento to
    jalapeno,
cauliflower and broccoli and oregano and basil, and not to
    forget
the flowers: statice and asters and zinnias and nicotianas:

the every morning watering and soil inspections,
the farewell to the frost, the rototilling, the spreading
of horse manure, stringing rows and staking, hoeing
and weeding, the tucking-in with last year's straw.
It's time to plant, you said, holding the rocky dirt in your hand,
when it sifts through our fingers. When it unshapes itself.
The way I unshape myself

on this haybale. My study is a wheatfield. These words
are birdsong. Dawn is the title of this book, leaves
rustling near an open window. I record as it passes
the spring. Spider webs quivering in the apple tree.
Redwing blackbirds and robins and wrens architecting
their hidden palaces. I make certain commitments
about my future. I dwell on a song as it sparrows to the
    beanfield

and back again to its branch. My loved ones are twigs
and straw and deerhair I clasp in my mouth
to weave the nest that surrounds my dying. Ganya.
We are bulbs of light   say these young onions
we are wet with dew   say the early rose buds.
Says the mourning dove's flight out of the spruce tree.
In our beings we are brilliant.

Look up and examine the woman in the garden.
Her hands are soil in a raised bed. Consider the corridor
of light, the squirrel's scuttle on the beech tree,
teaching us to love our ties to their last splendor.
Consider the hummingbird, who demonstrates how to tread
the air, the way he flickers, not as the buzzard
who swirls slowly over the roadkill, or even as the butterfly

in constant flutter like a flower petal wind-tossed,
but among these hollyhocks and sweet williams, pausing
and posing, silent, staring into my face as if to suggest:
You are not yet a flower. You cannot fill me with delight.
We allow time to whiten us. To make us familiar
as this now summer grass, the turning constellations.
Beyond the fiftieth gate of reason, the quietudes,

the seventy faces of the Word, we stare into the miraculous,
our mouths slightly open, our eyes wet. Like Moses
through parted waters, we float across the air to our appointed
    tasks,
saints in our synagogue, chanting ancestral words.
As now, Sabbath dusk, a thin orange line seeps the horizon,
the crescent moon cradles its emptiness. Coffee.
Silence. The church across Scrubgrass gathers worshipers.

We sit on the porch swing and listen to the hymns, drifting
through a day of fluid time. Summer water. Sister and
  brother
toss the football, the older instructing the younger.
Their parents are singing jubilant for a life in heaven.
Beyond them, former congregants are already there,
their spirits marked by stones of various sizes and states
  of repair.
That's it, she says. *This way. See the spiral?*

They will play a long time before they enter the eastern door
of the white building and take their places in the pews and
  listen
to laughter much like their own through the open windows.
Now the garden flames a holy fire and the sky folds
its blue wings like a heron's in sleep. And even longer
before the western door opens and they settle in another life
beside their loved ones, who approach now, the service ended.

Four:

Sages

For Etheridge Knight

1
He was in the shower
and fifteen minutes late.
I could hear him drying off

and singing. My business
was to make sure he got there,
but I thought he'd think I was

just another white college
professor who didn't know
his work well enough.

An empty bottle on the dresser,
butts smashed into saucers.
Papers strewn on the mattress.

The stories: how he was strung out
and a thief and lived on the streets
of nowhere like Indianapolis.

How he had to visit the university
earlier than planned
so he could beat the cancer.

He stepped out, wrapped
in a towel—yes, I saw the leg,
scarred almost down to the bone,

blue with clots and pus:
Got it when a car hit me.
Dragged me clear ten feet.

2

He is spotlit,
amplifying what he says
about the oral tradition,

voice like the slivers
between the rails and crossties
after a train glides past:

poets speaking to be heard,
different from a page lying
flat in silence, but the spoken

is song, voice to ear, is history.
The voice is jailcell and splash
of light on the floor, is dope

and fucked up. It's balls
and snatch, brick and blood,
cracking with smoke and drink.

It's croak and spit and smooth
slide and cry in the words
it croons about its daughter.

3
I was in the joint once. Not
as him, but doing time
in my own way, teaching

composition for rent money.
Summer drought, sweat
staining like a second skin,

dust swirling across the yard.
Class was one level below
the gym where chests spurted

grunts and heaves, quick breaths,
animal strains, pounding,
groans from the stress.

No office hours. Each was awarded
two days off their sentence
for perfect attendance.

Walls were cracked like veins,
cigarette butts stomped out
into small black splotches.

They wrote about their trials,
some developing how they were wronged,
others the details of their penance,

and the way the curves,
undersides of their ladies'
thighs, would give way, at 3 a.m,

alone in their cells, stroking
their own small hairs. One
looked me straight in the eyes:

I killed someone.
You teach me good
because I'm gonna write me a book.

4

During a break, a few of them
were gathered in a circle
around a baby starling who dropped

from behind a drainpipe, a small
pool of oil on the pavement,
its black tissues shuddering,

wingbones snapped. Back inside,
in their mandatory blue shirts,
they brainstormed freedom,

their words white chalk on blackboard:
sky, woman, space. And now
they tell me he's dead, no

surprise, considering the system.
This is close as I can get, Etheridge,
not enough, the other side of the bars.

Guards wait outside the door
of this room without acoustics,
where we read our private scratchings, aloud.

For Irina Ratushinskaya

I went in a healthy woman. But they took care of that.
Citing one of her poems as evidence, seven years.

Spare lines about wearing the body's rags before god.
She is thinning down to muscle. Solitary

can't shut her up—she scrapes with her nails
verses into scraps of soap,

recites each poem like someone
who writes what she herself is afraid to read.

She rinses the bar clean and flushes it down
into the sewers. The authorities never search below
   the surface.

The poems pile up, so many she has to remember—
the titles, the order: ten, twenty-five, a hundred,

two hundred and fifty, eyes fixed into a thick
wall, chanting over and over in her head a rosary of words,

a *Hassid* davening in the blank face of her own execution.
It's not difficult. It's my calling. They are smuggled out,

one by one, a whispering of alliteration and assonance,
smooth touch of vowels, soft sibilance from cellmate's lips

into cellmate's ear, heart by heart, the words passed
in memorized passage all the way into the West.

In Cather Country

The train depot is preserved, the way
she saved the voices of the pioneers
who rode these rails that now hold no locomotion
but still connect distance with distance.

Tonight the town is at the stockcar races—
Red Cloud, marked off in each direction
by a metal sculpture of a plow against
prairie and sky, all she saw, arriving

like an immigrant, like Antonia,
the one you swear she fell in love with,
and used a male's voice to disguise herself,
the way she'd dress and act like a man,

hair kept short, white shirt and black tie,
studying to be a doctor, signing her name *William*.
Her house—still the original color. Inside,
the ceramic baking bowls and farm tools,

the small deathbed of her grandmother who
came first and built a hut when the land
was the geographical center of nowhere.
And the attic: "like a hospital ward,"

impossible, this August drought, to breathe in,
her closed-sized room sealed behind Plexiglas
so we can observe the surviving dust,
where she studied, hours deep as the horizon,

Greek and biology, and where, staring
into a sky empty and vast as her earth,
its other half, its pool, the first spiritings
of the possibilities for beauty stirred.

We are told that each time Willa returned,
she requested a horse and buggy and rode down
the dirt paths of her childhood, meandering
through scrubgrass and bluffs to the divide,

visiting the Norwegian cemetery to touch
the soil that would bury her characters.
And what else had she but the crescendo
of the wind and space opening into more space

into more space? She said when she moved
from Virginia she took one look
into each direction and felt erased.
But she wrote herself back into the land.

The engines at the Raceway screech and roar,
around and around go the youth of Nebraska,
the sun pouring down its orange water over the farms,
flooding the plains gold, the crop, what's left of it.

Upon Leaving Martins Ferry, Ohio

for James Wright

The late November grass
holds onto its green,
layers the small hills
that rise and fall

like Indian mounds.
The sky is blue
as the eyes of Jesus
who hangs in Salvation

Army windows on every
main street along this
Bible belt. We listened
to you breathe in

deep and slowly release
the smoke, gray as the river
below your hometown.
Your hand twitched, the ash

lengthened as you lost
yourself in your own words,
speaking of the state
I'm looking out into:

I still dream of home.
We are in the same myth.
And we who want to die
an easy death will abandon

our bodies to the cancer
in a hospital far from home.
Everybody back in Columbus
is watching the game. If we win,

we'll tear down the goalposts,
spill out in one body
like a cult caught up in a ritual,
in love with each other, briefly.

English as a Second Language

1

It's been raining for days
in this false spring of late winter.
Animals, half-conscious, crawl
their way back to the surface.
The Cambodians hunt for worms.
Coming out of their houses, another
day long with unemployment,
they drive to the Olentangy River,
muddy in the gray twilight,
and with their hands burrow
into brown soil, soft as soup,
their fingers inching deeper
for the copper to sell at Bob's
Bait and Tackle, ten dollars
a pail, crammed to the edge.

2

two cups of rice per day   two
with water   more like a drink
so i catch fish   sneak into woods
i eat leaves off trees   teacher
run in high grass to mountain
get food for family   work very hard
no leave because father   mother
afraid to cross river
when we swim mekong   teacher
water take us   to columbus ohio

3

I recite tenses for repetition:
run, ran, eat, ate,
saying the past is what happened
before, last night, another place.
They are quiet around the table
looking into books at pictures
of stoves, sinks, refrigerators.
Smoke rises from men's hands until
lost among the fluorescent lights
flickering on the green ceiling.
A young voice, Chaunpaul's, sings
in her high-pitched language,
sounds that fall and bend like water,
as if she no longer had parents,
and her children will be lost in strange lives.

Child of God

We were drawn by the starlings
who dropped their waste
over everyone's head

but nevertheless flew
through the crazy air
to their own kind

a little later each evening
and filled maple and elm
like purple leaves, sounding

the ember dusk, those
thousands of nuisances.
March, late afternoon,

half-blue, half-orange sky,
small patches of snow
still melting

into the shadowed lawns,
our false spring
before the final blizzard.

In the temporary warmth
we cut class, pitched
pennies against the Church

of the Assumption. The way
you guided a pinball
to just that spot of flipper,

you followed your coin
as it spun
within an inch

of the transubstantiation.
I know what it's like here,
you said, pointing to the wall.

*I want to know what it's like
there: a true child of God,*
your eyes so wide with belief

you were half-way already.
                    Now,
the man with his science says

it's all biochemical
and nothing can save you,
not even the lithium. Soon

the concentration will go little
by little into the other world.
After dark the authorities

blasted them out,
over our heads wings pulsating
with their smaller explosions.

What Survives

1

We discovered them, so many
years ago, above the Hocking River
and beyond the barbed wire fence,
behind the dark institution—

its white columns from the Civil War,
Ohio Gothic, black iron crisscrossed
over windows, widow's walks
where generation after generation

of pigeons gather to roost
and coo their absurd music,
tunnels connecting each
building like a sewage system

of lost volunteers and patients
rotting in the distance beyond
their screams, torture chambers
in the cellar: the racks,

the tubs of water that freezes
and scalds them back into sanity.
And, on the other side, the apple trees,
where, late autumn afternoons,

we picked only the ripe ones
until the trees blazed orange
and the harvest moon shooed
us away, our sacks overfilled,

all we could carry home.
Only once did we remain, remove
our shoes, sneak into the grounds,
you leading the way, knowing

when to be quiet and when
to walk, how to hold the pricker
vine between thumb and fore-
finger so it wouldn't slash my skin.

We followed a narrow patch
of earth into an abandoned
courtyard strewn with weeds
and bushes and there they were:

the headstones, hardened
with the dirt they were breaking
back into, scattered haphazardly
in a circle, mounds facing inward,

the skeletons sealed against the sane.
We searched for names, dates—
only, barely readable in the mud-gray,
number after number after number.

Sparrows fed in the hairline cracks.
You imagined stories, identified
the anonymous bones: Fred
Griffith, who shot his family

when the crop went bad,
Saddy Hatchett, who stared
and stared out of her window
for years. As we were leaving,

you turned around in a last look,
stood quiet and, like someone
who could see his future, broke
into a kind of dance.

2
You get on a train,
see a beautiful woman
sitting alone next
to a window, blanket

warming her lower body.
The evening sun glares
her hair yellow as the wheat
she is looking out into.

Her face is soft and blushed.
You sit next to her, wanting
to talk out your troubles.
But she is memorizing

the landscape, fields
and more fields,
the earth repeating itself.
Before the breakdown every limb

was twitching and your eyes
glared past whoever it was
who tried to speak to you.
The train grows dark.

Soon she is asleep, her head
on an arm she'd propped
in the space between her seat
and the window. You wonder

what your friends will say
when they understand
you've left again, gone crazy,
took a walk to clear your head

and wound up in California.
Suddenly you feel soft breathing.
Asleep, she has rolled over:
her face is barely touching yours

as it glides down
until it rests on your shoulder.
She lifts her still-closed eyes,
slightly, pressing her lips

against your ear, smoothing
her tongue all along its valleys.
You brush her hair back.
The train slows into a station

and she pulls away, looks
back out the window, the plains
in the depths of her face.
The lights flicker on.

Two porters, one with a chair,
arrive at your compartment.
They ask you to move aside.
They lift her, carry her away.

3

Now you live in this asylum.
Paint chips crackle the walls,
fall to the hard floor
like thousands of pieces

of angels' wings. We stalk
the corridors, box-shaped
room after box-shaped room,
you looking out of shattered windows

to measure where we are.
This is the building of the back wards,
closed down by the state
and deserted for half a century.

I can slip in here, you say,
when they think I'm somewhere else,
leading me to the wrought-iron
staircase that spirals us to the loft—

everywhere pigeon skeletons,
their bones wholly in place,
dispersed about the attic
in accidental gracefulness,

layered with feathers and dust,
some smaller ones prostrate
between halves of their worn shells,
membranes insubstantial as air,

as if too frail for the hatching.
You repeat the legend: *The patients
are still below us and if we're quiet
we can hear distinct voices*

sounding the abandoned spaces.
We pace softly, softly.
Listen. Now. Our hearts
beat back at us from the dark.

The Book of the World

April afternoon silence,
unbroken sky, water rippling, robins
and grackles in and out of the pines,
purple and yellow crocuses opening,

sap rising and this hunger,
green shoots of lilacs, red buds of maples,
earth oozing, light clinging a little longer,
cells proliferating beyond measure.

What's beauty but the signal of death?

Mary is expanding beyond herself.
Already what we thought was cut out
of her breast has reappeared
in her liver, her bones, her spinal cord—enough

of this abundance, this sun infusing
its bedazzlement down the spine of each tree,
spilling its seeds on the pond's surface.

And then the peepers,
tiny bells like gates opening
into another world.

All day I've been reading Hopkins.
I want to hear the thrush he heard,

whose song does so rinse and wring
the ear it strikes like lightenings to hear
him sing,

and perhaps I do hear,
but without knowing,
in the evening's imperceptible motions—
a ladder of sparrows, the dark,

then the comet everyone's caught up by,
star with a smear, a cape, star with a shroud.

Body or portent, on clear nights
it carries the cosmic closer
and we want it to signal something

like stepping into an empty room filled with light
pouring through our privacies.

We want this awe—
the angel above the earth or the one
who pulls from behind our hearts our losses.

A month ago Mary's face was beaming.
Her son Evan was chanting his portion
from the great Book about how God told Moses
he could not see His face.

But he can stand by a rock
and it would come to pass,
His glory would pass by and Moses
will see His back, but His face will not be seen.

The rabbi interpreted.
We cannot understand our lives as we live them.
Only in retrospect can we understand
how one event led to another.

And when Moses came out
of the mount, he knew not that the skin
of his face, by speaking with Him, shone.

Mary's hair is falling out.
Two tubes snake out of her chest
full of chemicals so toxic
she had to sign a waiver.

They take her to the death point,
then they try to bring her back.

Mary had golden hair, like in the fairy tale.
She was called Sister Mary Golden Hair Surprise
by someone who loved her.

I forgot my portion,
my place in the book of the world.
Though it comes round once a year,
like my birth, like my death.

On the day the child becomes an adult,
the parent becomes a child,
growing backward, toward the source.

And the child will carry this parent forever.

I will perform miracles, God told Moses,
in the great study on the other side,
at the desk floating in relentless blue.

ChemoMary, she calls herself. *Just a bad hair day.*

And the wings beat furiously silent above us.

Poem in Search of Perfection

I want to write the appropriate words
as they appear in their proper order,
no cross outs or syntax reversals, no

staring blankly at the blank page or
rubbing my hair back or getting out
of my chair and walking deep beyond

the next field until what needs said
formulates out of the chaos my mind is.
The word appropriate to the subject,

as in the Old School, anymore I can't
measure, the way my grandfather weighed
apples and bananas on his scale. Or

my grandmother, deaf, held one in each hand,
tiny in that enormous crowd. Gradually,
her hearing became so perfect she'd listen

only to the pure sound of her own voice.
I wish I could write the word forbidden
to be written, describe the face of the One

who will only show His back, shape the sounds
so they taste as truth tastes on the tongues
of the prophets. Let them provide the balance

and relieve my friends' misery like an embracing
water, unsay the diagnosis of the specialist
who obscened the air with the sentence:

No cure. Seven-year-old daughter, blonde
and surging with her own sweet life force.
Allow, Oh Arbitrators of Expression,

these phonemes to be the one enzyme missing
in her genes and thereby restore to whom
I love, common people, beautiful souls,

their workaday world and its normal order
again. Grant these pockets of air
to reverse time into last week, which was

our other life. The word always unsaid,
like the utterance that can never be taken
back. How our first speech marks our last

pronouncement. Nothing can be told against
this unspeakable grief. A child breaks down,
and all the languages invented add up to silence.

This Sweater

Stretching into my new used white sweater
I bought at an AIDS thrift shop
on Columbus Avenue in the West Seventies,

a slight coffee stain on the front,
a small hole on the bottom in the back,
lighter than a heavy coat,

heavier than a light coat,
perfect for this unexpected warmth
of early January, balmy as spring,

snug around the chest and arms,
I wonder who was the bulky man
with the fatal disease

warmed by this sheep's wool,
matching my measurements.
He wore it in but didn't wear it out,

then rejected it with everything else,
left to others, I hope to a lover,
to worry over and decide

not to keep, perhaps because
he couldn't stop touching its emptiness.
Rather a donation, passing it on

to another, to me. Not unusual
to inherit the garment of the dead
or to wonder if I also will acquire

a small portion of the wearer's soul,
we who are so similar in size,
sharing as we do the same taste

in our apparel. And if whoever loved him
happens to witness me now, fully
embraced in its warmth, still holding

its shape, is reminded
of that soul? And if that memory
makes him suddenly live again?

The Oldest Brother Lesson in the World

In the room without heat the desk's cherry wood
warmed his body all night until the pale skin of dawn

found his face pressed beside the book opened
to drawings of the skeleton he studied through

the noises of that house, the screams of our father
calling him down to dinner. Ten years younger,

upset with one crisis or another, I carved our name
in the surface but he said furniture is alive

like us if we allow it to breathe and pass it on
the way it was made. Near an open window he wore

the scratches away with steel wool, his fingers precise as if
treating bruises on skin, brushed on the stain

with delicate surgeon's eyes, the wet streaks shimmering
like roses in the sun. It was what he left me,

smudged with the invisible smoothing of his palms,
the imprint of his ghost-ear listening to the tree in the wood,

what I listen for now, sanding my own splinters
and chipped edges, the flaws he taught me to re-touch.

Some say as brothers get older they get more distant,
meaning we grow out of our childhoods,

when we sat naked in the same waters
and he rubbed my tender flesh with soap.

This will last for as long as memory lasts,
and now that it is here written down, longer,

and any one who cares can imagine an older
brother cleaning the younger as has been done

according to custom throughout the centuries.
It will last as long as the oldest brother lesson in the world
    will last,

the story our mother taught us about the two sons
who wound up wandering apart in two separate worlds.

Her own two brothers stopped speaking over something
or other and the years hammered the nails of their refusal

harder into their wounds until one died and became
bones that spoke less than the silence of the flesh.

Does his blood cry to his brother from the ground?
Is cursing a brother the same as cursing yourself?

Is looking into a brother's face like looking into water
and seeing your own death? Are brothers two wings

of a great bird? Does each carry inside of him the other
half of the secret of how to live a righteous life on earth?

Albert Einstein at the Soup Kitchen

Do I look like anyone? he asks,

as he swoops the long spoon into the peas,
lifts it a few inches
and holds it steady to pour
onto the tray of the next famished mouth,
shouts to George for more
as his supply empties down.

I'm the bread and donut man
in this assembly line of volunteers
who gather for our three hours
of weekly service and socialism:

Jose the finger-pointing Filipino
who pours the punch and repeats:
The wages of sin is death
and only reads Paradise from the Comedy,

for his description of heaven, he says, *and light;*

Jake the Buddhist, who scrapes the dishes
as they are returned, saves whatever
appears untouched for someone else's

insatiable hunger;
          Sal, who tells me he was on the other side
of the line, meaning he was one of the thousand
who form every morning single-file around this Church
of the Apostles, up 9th Avenue and around

28th Street,
   like the snake, he chants,
looking out the window beyond Crack Park,

cursed above the beasts of the city
to eat dust all the days of its life.

And their eyes are filled with dust,
                              drugged and sleepy,
bodies stiff from sidewalk cardboard sofas.

The peaman, it turns out, looks like Albert Einstein,
the shaggy white hair and white mustache,
pronounced nose and dark sad eyes.

I'm an actor, he explains. *They pay me to look like the genius.*

He shows me his card: $e=mc^2$:
Equity equals many characters,

and I'm honored to be near even the resemblance of the man—
not because I understand relativity
and the contradicting theories of light,

but because of how steady he is with the spoon,
filling each helping to the brim,
as if each portion should be equal and abundant.

The Scribe

"The golden-winged bird who pierces an opening
into the egg of the world."

—Simone Weil

1

How can we tell a body in pain? Down any avenue,
say Broadway, mid-summer, mid-day: the flashy and the quick,
the overcoated minister talking trush for a dollar, the beer-
    can-covered

unicyclist, ring in the teenager's tongue, the spiked and
    the flecked,
the nail in the wrist of the accordion-playing-for-God
    minister, severed
brilliantly against the skyscrapers. The blades and windows

of longing, the aromatherapy palace and the $2-a-palm
    psychic, the lump
on the breast, the shell game on the cardboard box, the
    jolting and wailing
and dealing, birds encased in plastic, trees growing through
    plaster.

Not the heart's ache only, memory of the pulled-back hair,
    your mother's
exploding laughter, but the packed subway car, the elevator
    shaft. If only
the updraft of winter birds, the long snow descending. If only
    the ancestral

woodsmoke, the huddling. Once it was possible to walk uphill.
Once it was possible to hold the taste of the wooden spoon
   on your tongue.
It's the visionary on the corner waving his book. It's the man
   who is a torso

and a tin-cup-in-his-mouth against the doorway of the
   famous cinema,
pockets of our lives sewn on the inside of his violin case
   where neither gold
nor silver accompany our departure nor precious pearls. It's
   the woman

beside us mouthing words into a camera for a film they will
   edit us out of,
the lovers spewing on the sidewalk, the second-story opera
   singer vocalizing.
We shape ourselves into hard forms to make a career out of death.
   Rest

assured: we will not be cut or scrutinized nor will the juices be
   drained.
We will not be left unattended, psalms recited, white
   garments sewn.
We will sift into the earth in unpolished pine with holes the
   size of dust

and someone will place a small stone if only a groundskeeper
or the ordained one or the wind carrying sand from the great
   city.
Woe another hour has gone. Rest assured. Someone is setting
   this all down.

2

In the narrow store on Essex Street, for example, an ancient
   scribe-
of-the-Book crouches before a scroll laid out like a stretched
   sheet
on the splintered wooden counter, shadowed from the evening
   glare.

He clutches a quill plucked from a kosher goose, its indelible
   black ink
prepared from vegetables, and inscribes onto the dead flesh of
   a goat
the inspired and accounted-for words and letters and if he
   misspells or slips

or jerks he fasts and purifies himself in clear water and starts
   again,
this chronicler of the Holy of Holies, oracular, tall and thin,
   bearded and established,
white ear-locks, cap pinned to white hair, peering over the
   parchments

threaded like pieces of cloth for a gown or a shroud, each cell
and bone of him inflamed, his handwriting steady as if
   stitching skin to skin,
his eyes staring onto the white surface as if into a door they
   could open,

as if his fixed attention could trace the script into a
   perfection so singular
it will be memorized and recited before the people for another
   century—

the agonies and dream-visions, the propagations and
   prognostications,

the secret codes and numbers and wonders and hidden
   correspondences
that will puzzle and saturate, savage and perplex, ravishing,
   furious,
in this city where we are forced to look every which way for
   our lives.

In this city where we walk down Broadway from the
   celebrated hospital,
dazed and silent and solicitous in the sidewalk explosion of
   watches and smoke.
To be the color of dead leaves, like certain unnoticed insects.
   To desire

nothing more than to be alone. To witness the cardinal's
   blood-red flight
out of the sweetgum tree, the snow falling, alive in its
   mission, into a curious
happiness, the misty distance, a small place, a dust mote in a
   cow's eye.

Or to be a junco, the sunflower seed it pecks at in the frozen
   earth,
or a mottled grouse, its inconspicuous song, its thrumming
   wings.
Or the golden-winged bird who pierces an opening into the
   egg of the world.

The House of Sages

I paused before The House of Sages,
beside the boarded-up synagogue,
on my walk down East Broadway

toward the river for relief
from the heat's tidal wave.
Founded in 1922, the slab stone says,

the year of my father's birth.
The white sign above the caged
door announces in Hebrew

the Polish *shtetl* of its origin.
Near the bolt lock and intercom
a spray of white paint:

swirls and loops like lopsided
hearts and question marks
and the street's fevered talk.

Through the cracked window
men in black were poring
dusty faces over pages spread

open like stilled wings,
quivering bodies revealed
in this afternoon glare shafting

the Lower East Side. I wanted
to enter there, to assume
the white robe and crown, to bow

down low before the open Ark
and touch the Book
with my scarf and place my fingers

to my lips and kiss there.
I wanted all of this, to arrive
and hear my name called,

son of my father, in the first
language and all the silence after.
I stood in the sidewalk's fire.

The gate opened. A bearded shadow
appeared and I stole inside
before it closed like a cloud behind me.

I peeked into the sanctuary
of the sacred and a sage
was reading a newspaper

the way my father or I myself
relaxed at table, long legs
stretched out on the dark oak,

feet crossed. Another
was solving a crossword puzzle,
inquiries in the holy tongue.

What questions down?
What questions across?
Were the answers printed

in the next life? A few
were bending their torsos
down and up, down and up,

as if lettering with their bodies
some unfathomable word
or testing out a new law of physics:

If you rub flesh with air, a spark.
Soon, first one then another
turned toward my direction,

all staring, eyes fixed, curious
at my intrusion. Should they touch
their foreheads to the eastern wall

or call the police? Briefly all the noise
of New York became one word
which filled the room, our only world.

G-d

Not even in representation, figure
or shape, nothing we can imagine
or create, no structure or sound or phrase—

not even symbols or color, formulas
or equations, nothing we can mold—
what we are incapable of calling out

or writing down. Our houses
are candles and stained glass,
in our pantries scrolls of words

we kiss and dance before.
The presence of beauty is without form,
and so the middle letter is erased,

spelling a word we can never pronounce,
our tongues stumbling for a vowel,
a syllable forbidden to be said,

for the sound itself is only a sign
of the original silence.
And what is it but silence after all,

the spaces we fill in with our prayers,
our actions with blessings? Here,
each of our images is graven

as we crave and carve your name
in our lower case, our imaginations
sealed in museums, wrung out in metal

and glass and stone, bound in ink
and cloth, where words follow
in their necessity out of the place

they fade into, as us, shaping the air
with our skins full of breath and bones
that become earth, walk, and are perfect.

Photo by Christine Hood

About the Author

Philip Terman was born in Cleveland, Ohio, and studied at Ohio University, The University of Washington, and Ohio State University. He is currently an Associate Professor of English at Clarion University of Pennsylvania. He initiated the literary and arts journal, *The Oil City Review,* and The Bridge Coffee House, a performance space in Franklin, PA, that is a gathering place for writers, musicians, and artists. His poetry has been published in numerous journals, including *Poetry, The Kenyon Review, The New England Review,* and *Tikkun Magazine.* He has received the Anna Davidson Rosenberg Award for Poetry on the Jewish Experience, an Academy of American Poets Prize, The Kenneth Patchen Award, and his poetry collection, *What Survives,* received The Sow's Ear Chapbook Prize in 1993. He lives in a converted one-room red-brick schoolhouse outside of Grove City, Pennsylvania with his wife, Christine Hood, and his daughter, Miriam.

Other Titles by MAMMOTH books